The Little Golden

WORDS

BY SELMA LOLA CHAMBERS

HORACE MANN SCHOOL, ST. LOUIS, MISSOURI

Illustrated by Gertrude Elliott

SIMON AND SCHUSTER · NEW YORK

THE LITTLE GOLDEN BOOKS ARE PREPARED UNDER THE SUPERVISION OF

MARY REED, Ph.D.

FORMERLY OF TEACHERS COLLEGE, COLUMBIA UNIVERSITY

THIS IS A BRAND-NEW BOOK, WRITTEN AND ILLUSTRATED ESPECIALLY FOR GOLDEN BOOKS

Introduction

It is fascinating for very young children to associate a word with its pictorial representation.

In THE LITTLE GOLDEN BOOK OF WORDS, each small picture represents a specific word. Full-page pictures in color are used to expand many of the ideas included in each group of words. For instance, a simple, labeled, detailed drawing of the family shows each individual member. On the opposite page the family is shown at the dinner table. In this picture the child will be able to name many objects in addition to the members of the family. Many other word groups—Things That Grow, Things That Go, Numbers, and so forth—are similarly treated. Children will enjoy finding pictures of familiar objects and activities.

THE LITTLE GOLDEN BOOK OF WORDS is intended to be used also by children who are just learning to read. They will soon begin to associate the written symbols with the pictures.

This book offers many opportunities for games in word recognition and spelling. If left to the spontaneous use of young children, it is likely to lead to a great variety of activities.

The Child

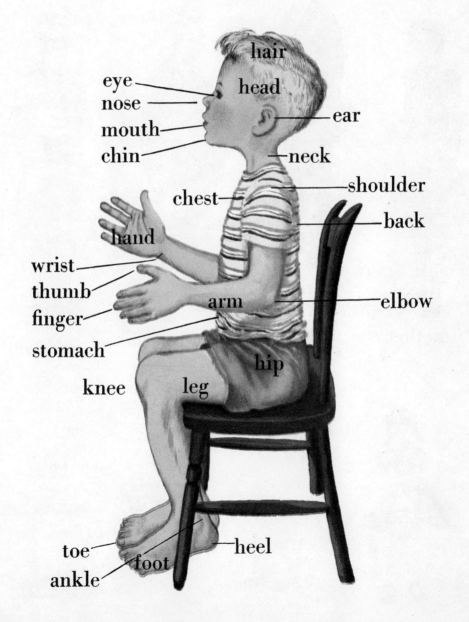

The Family

mother

father

grandfather

grandmother

sister

brother

baby

Clothes

coat

hat

cap

boots

dress

suit

handkerchief

gloves

stockings

snowsuit

sweater

socks

rubbers

mittens

pants

pajamas

earmuffs

beads

overalls

slippers

shoes

People

boy   girl   man   woman   children

they   she   he

Things That Grow

tree

flower

bush

strawberry

flower

tree

fern

corn

mushrooms

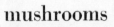

grass

Colors

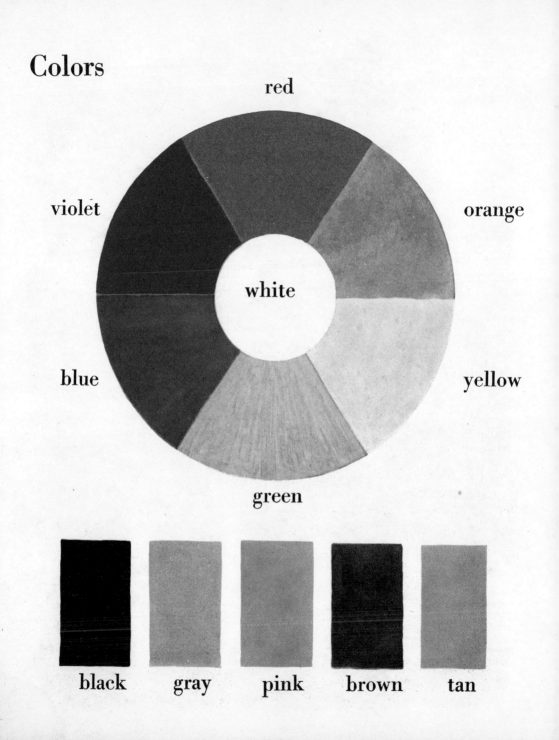

Shapes and Sizes

round

star

square

triangle

short

long

heart

tall

short

fat

thin

big

little

Animals

rabbit

pig

dog

cat

horse

sheep

deer

fox

goat

turtle

monkey

snake

lion

squirrel

cow

bear

elephant

mouse

fish

frog

Numbers

1 one

2 two

3 three

4 four

5 five

6 six

7 seven

8 eight

9 nine

10 ten

11 eleven

12 twelve

13 thirteen

14 fourteen

15 fifteen

16 sixteen

17 seventeen

18 eighteen

19 nineteen

20 twenty

The Alphabet

A apple

B bell

C cat

D dog

E egg

F fish

G grapes

H hat

I iron

J jar

K kite

L leaf

M mittens

N nest

O owl

P pear

Q queen

R rabbit

S school

T table

U umbrella

V valentine

W wagon

X xylophone

Y yarn

Z zebra

Birds

robin

pigeon

parrot

canary

sparrow

chick

hen

goose

gosling

duck

owl

woodpecker

turkey

rooster

sandpiper

swallow

penguin

crow

hummingbird

eagle

Things We Use

chair

table

bed

dishes

radio

book

box

basket

knife

broom

paper

crayons

fork

iron

spoon

pencil

glass

clock

rake

paints

pan

towels

pail

scissors

toothbrush

Things to Eat

bread

butter

jelly

eggs

milk

meat

cake

cheese

honey

cookies

rolls

pie

pudding

nuts

candy

pancakes

ice cream

More Things to Eat

apple

orange

carrot

peach

grapes

potato

cabbage

radishes

peas

beans

tomato

corn

celery

beet

onion

lettuce

pear

grapefruit

cherries

banana

plum

pineapple

Things to Play with

ball

wagon

marbles

rocking horse

kite

Teddy bear

sled

blocks

teapot

cup

balloon

drum

doll

bubble pipe

horn

jacks and ball

tricycle

jumping rope

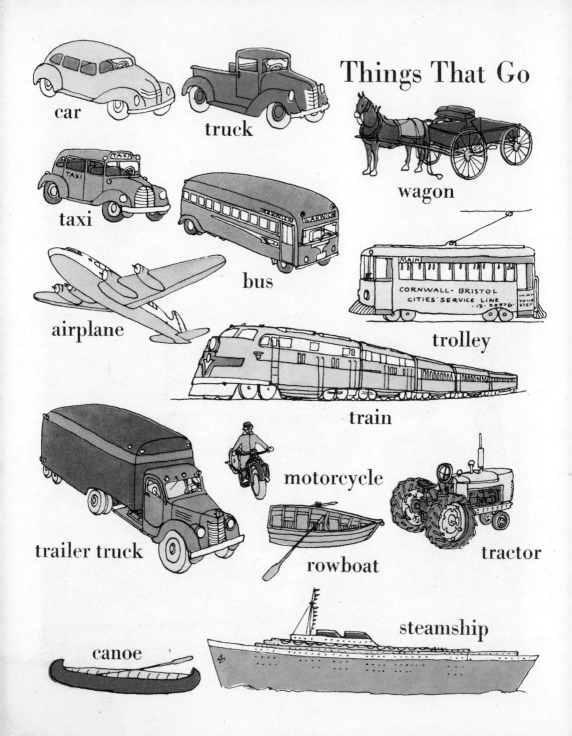

car

truck

Things That Go

wagon

taxi

bus

airplane

trolley

train

trailer truck

motorcycle

rowboat

tractor

steamship

canoe

Things We Do

work

jump

build

dance

run

swim

walk

eat

draw

crawl

swing

read

sleep

write

play

Word Helpers

to
the store

from
the store

stop

go

above
the clouds

below
the clouds

in
the house

out
of the house

over
the fence

under
the fence

empty

full

**up
the stairs**   **down
the stairs**   **socks on**   **socks off**

**yes, it is
raining**   **no, it is not
raining**   **before
the haircut**   **after
the haircut**

**many
fish**   **few
fish**   **old
shoes**   **new
shoes**

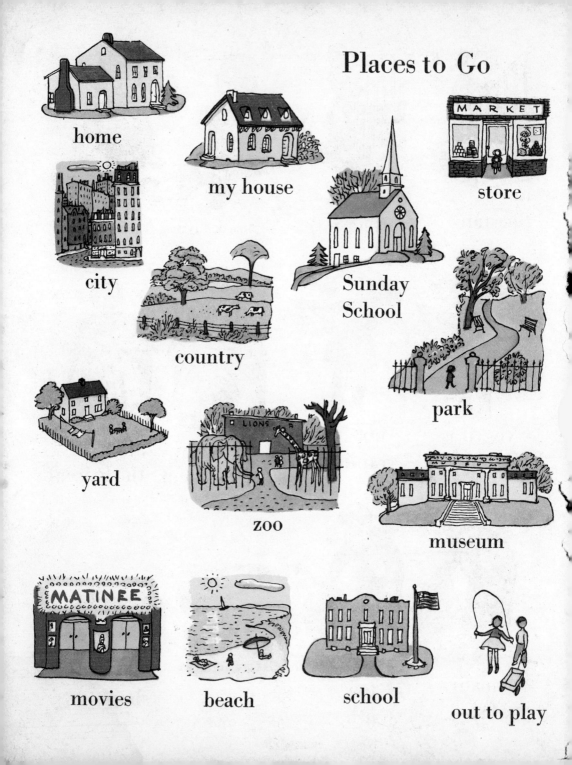

Places to Go

home

my house

store

city

country

Sunday School

park

yard

zoo

museum

movies

beach

school

out to play